Dream Homes

Really Cool Colouring **Book 1**

First published in 2015 by Kyle Craig Publishing

Text and illustration copyright © 2015 Kyle Craig Publishing

Editor: Alison McNicol

Design: Julie Anson

ISBN: 978-1-908-707-51-2

A CIP record for this book is available from the British Library.

A Kyle Craig Publication

www.kyle-craig.com

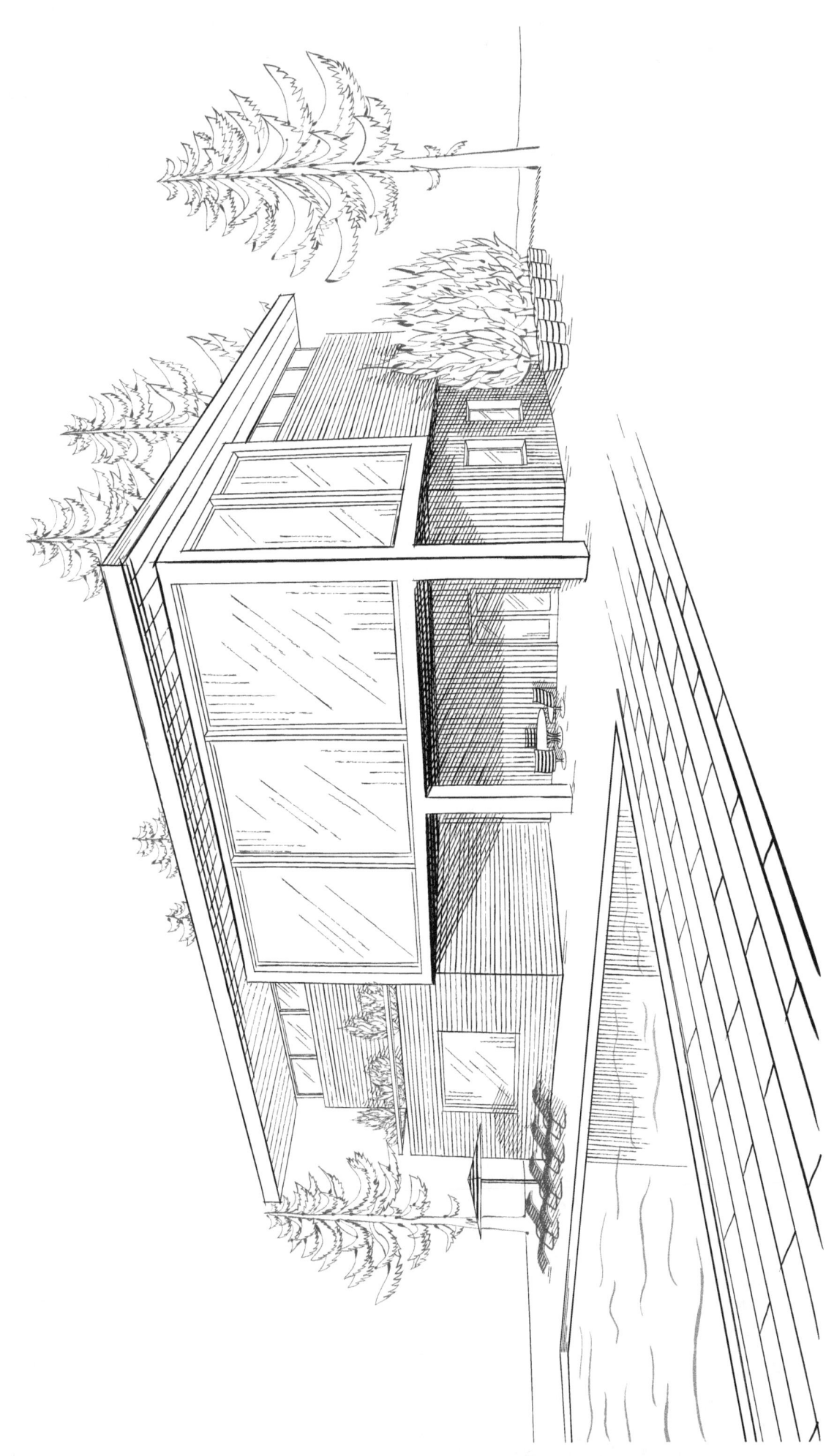

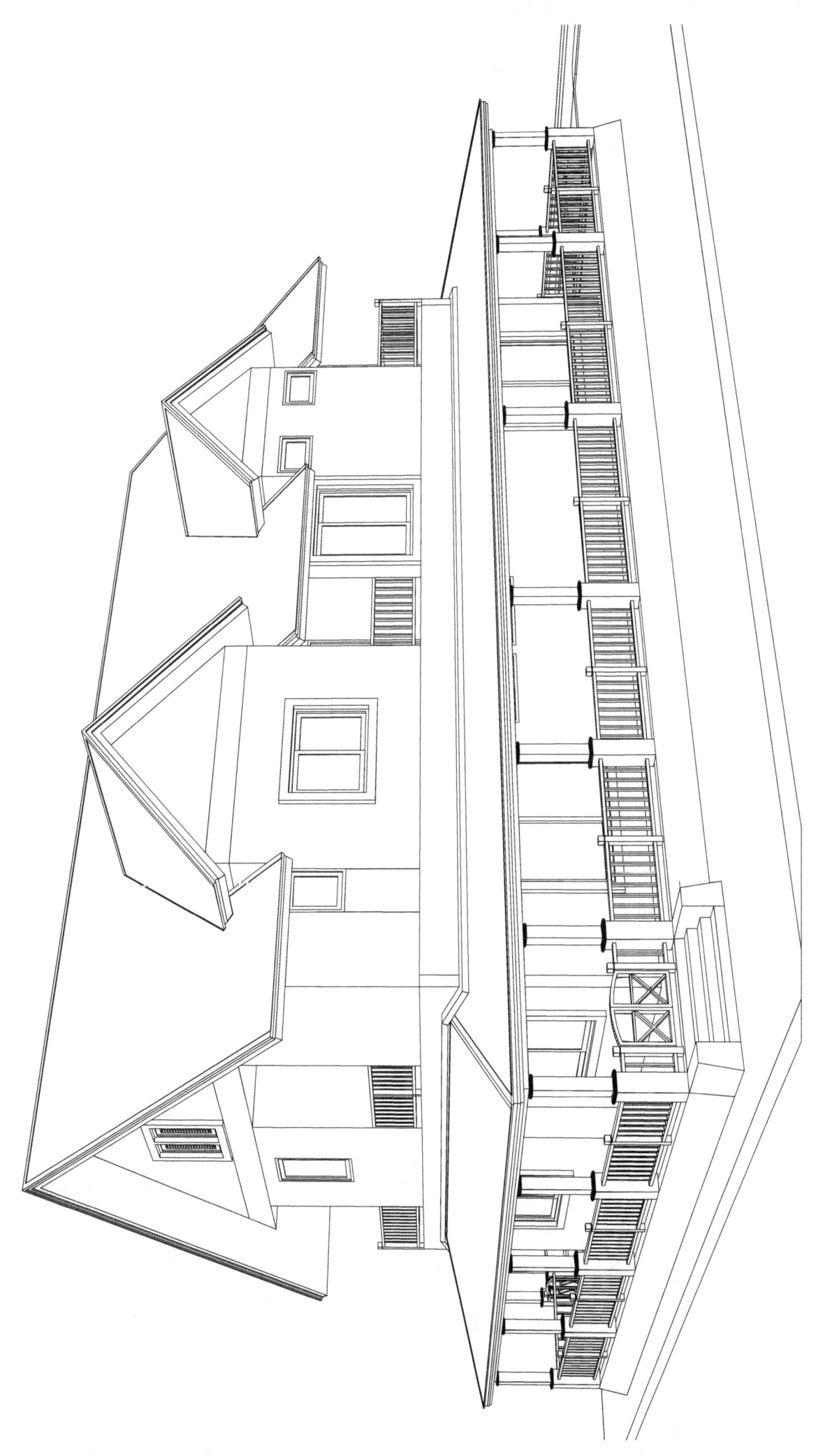

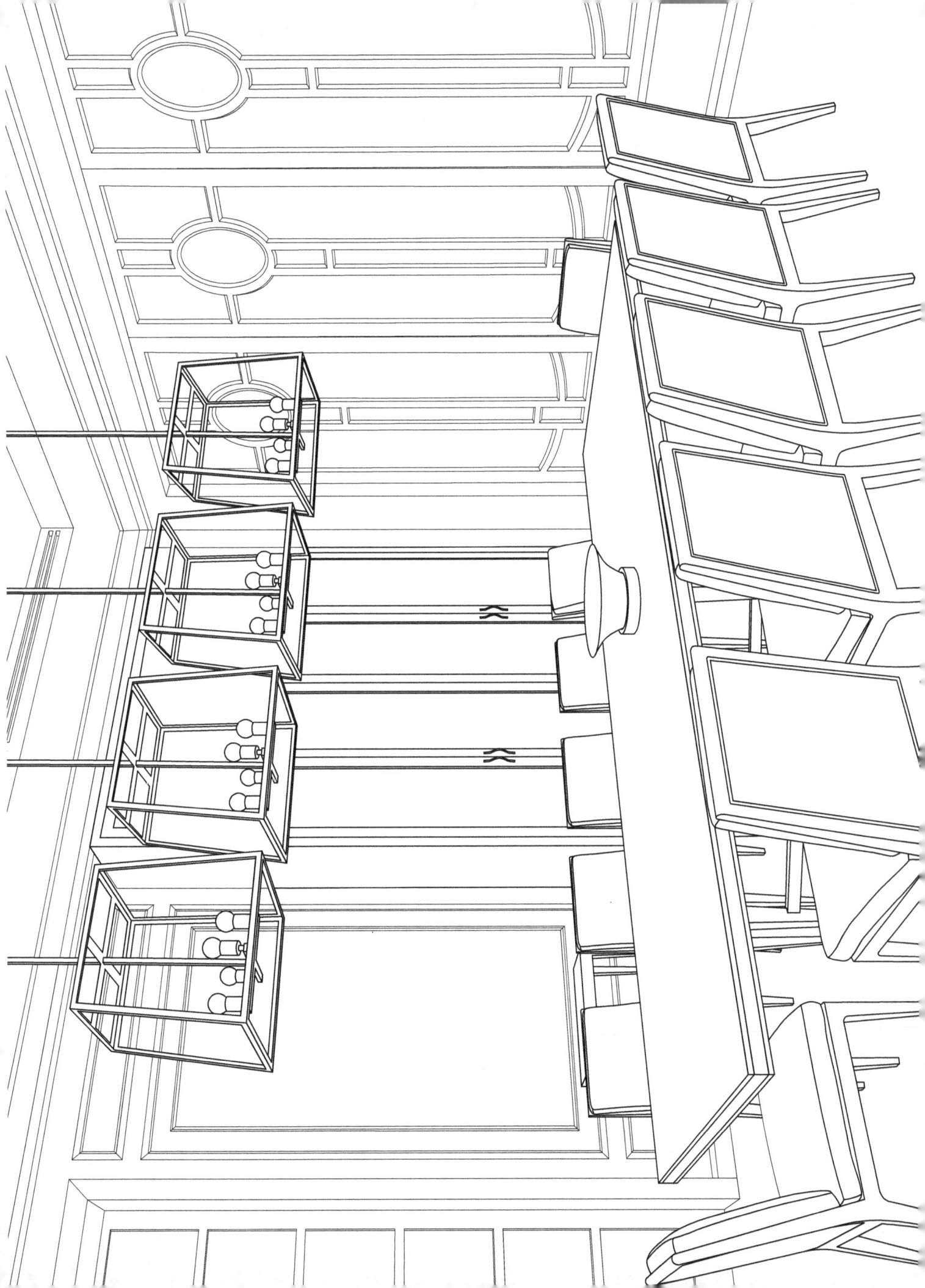

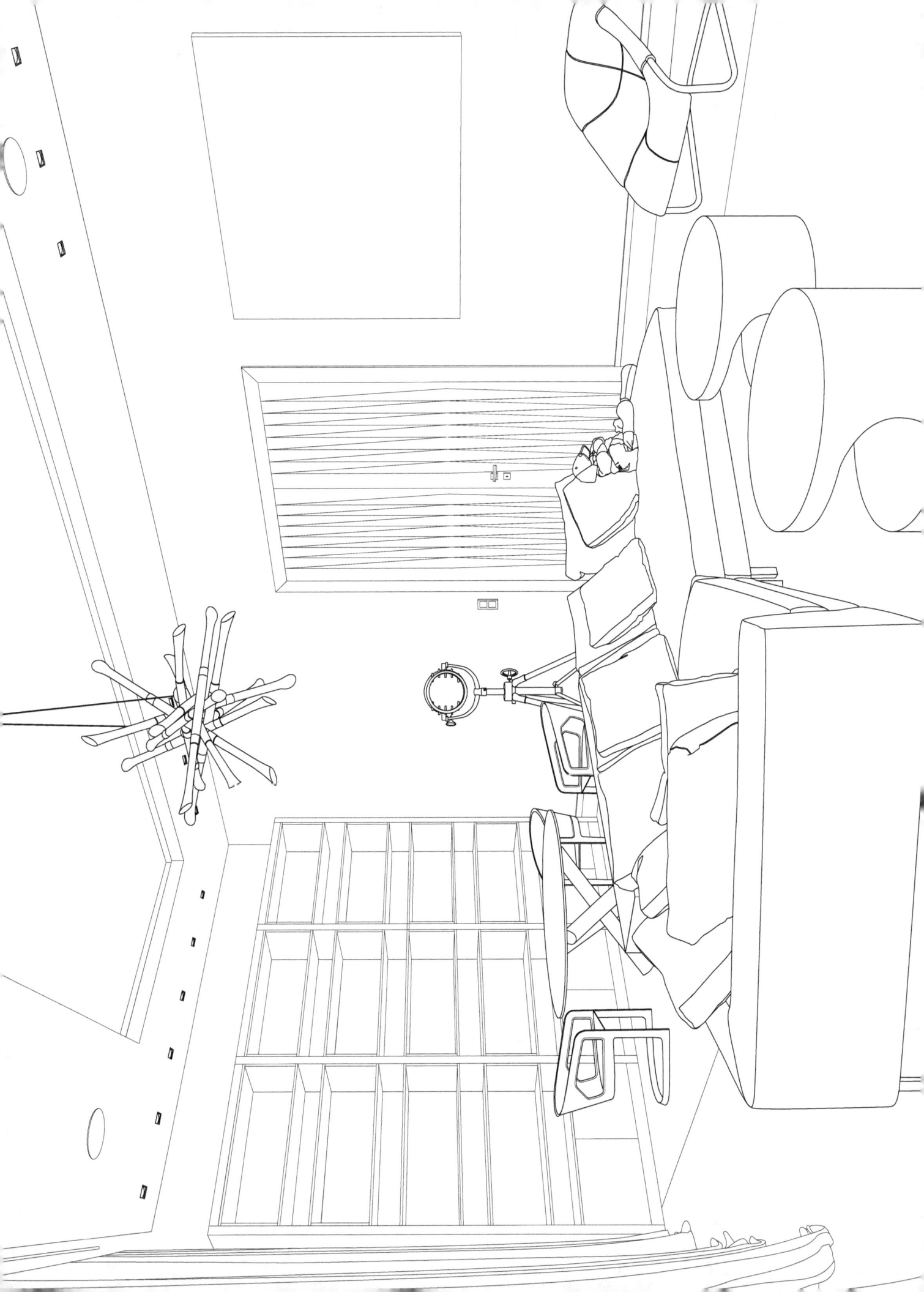

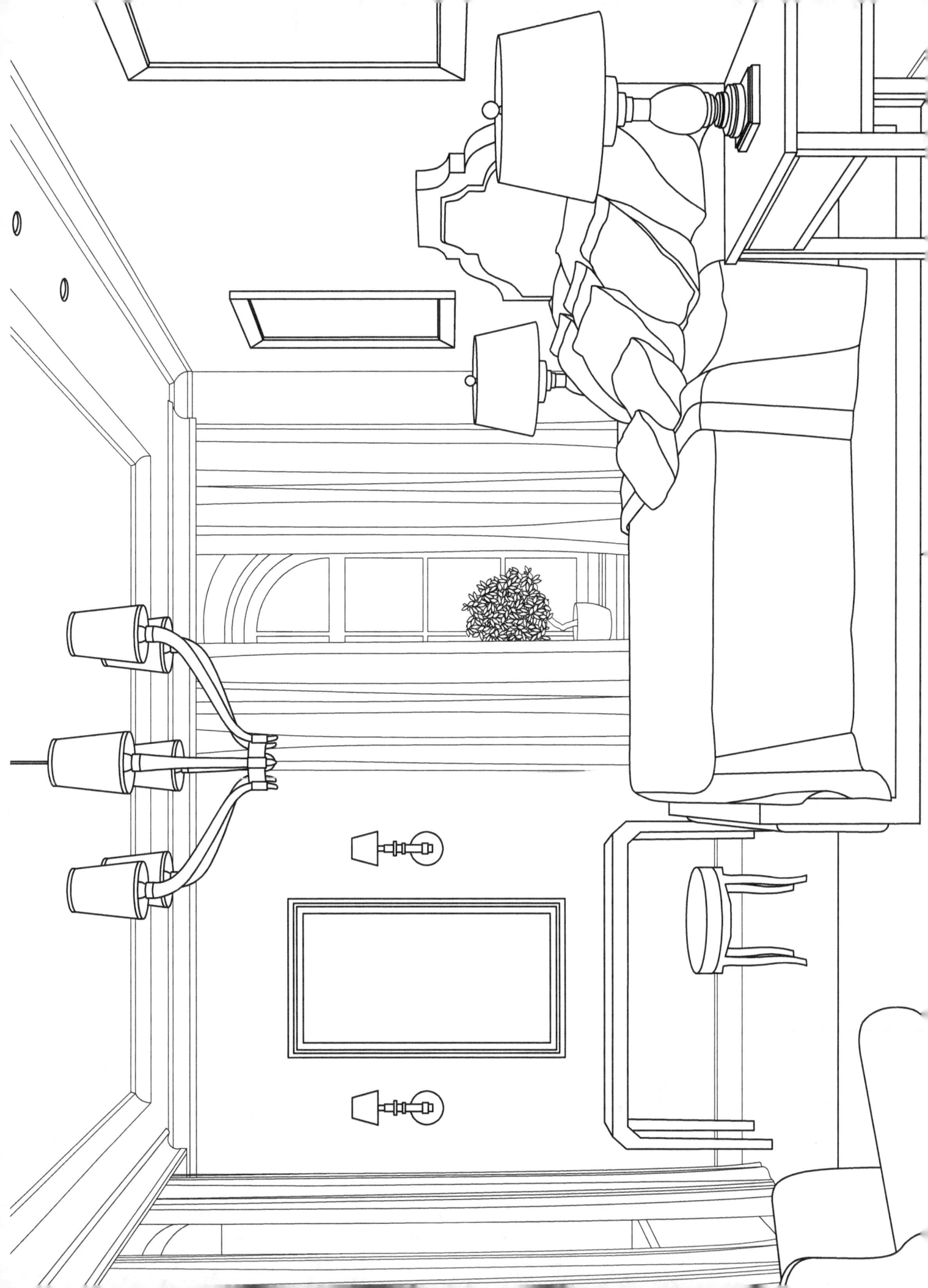

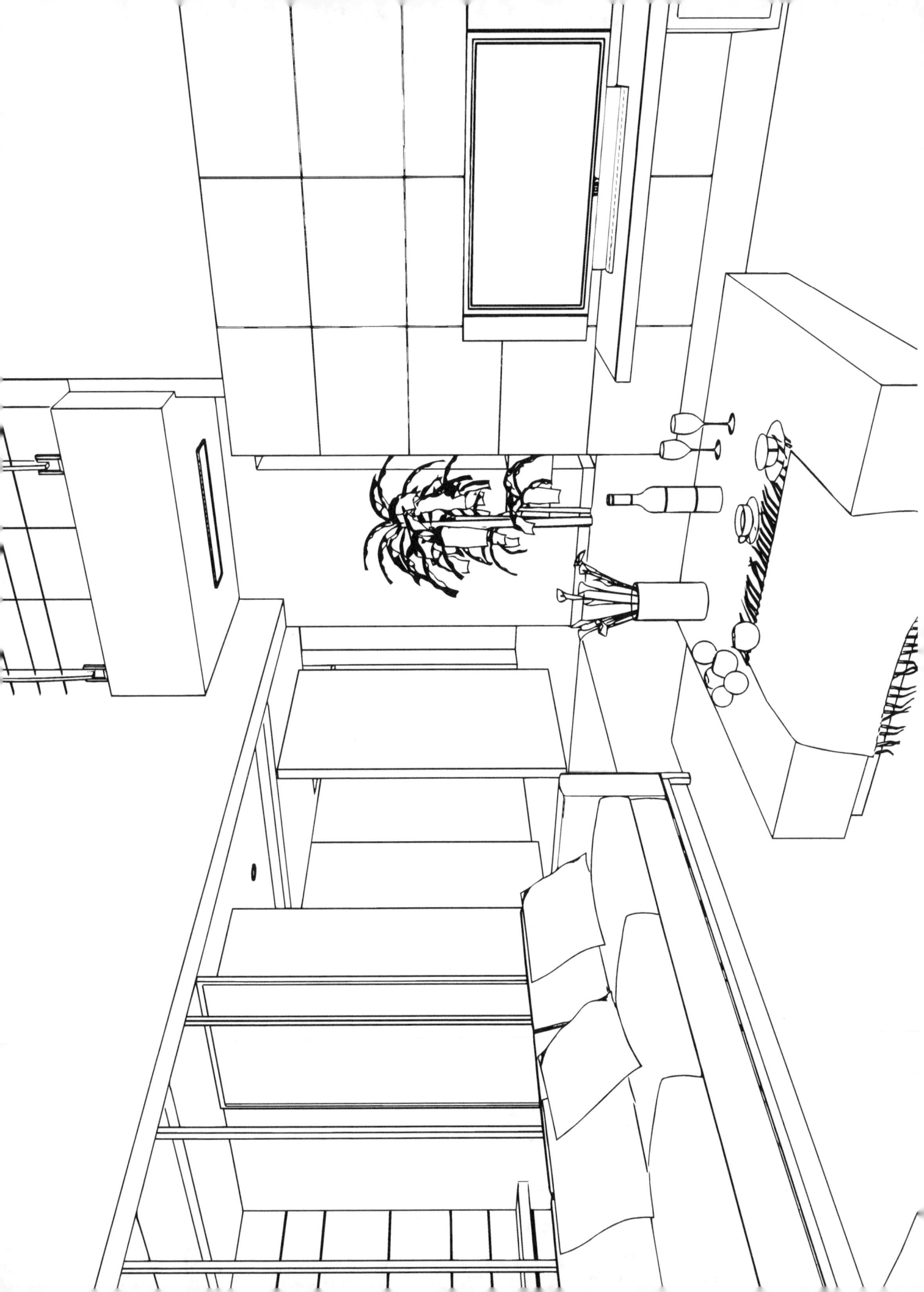

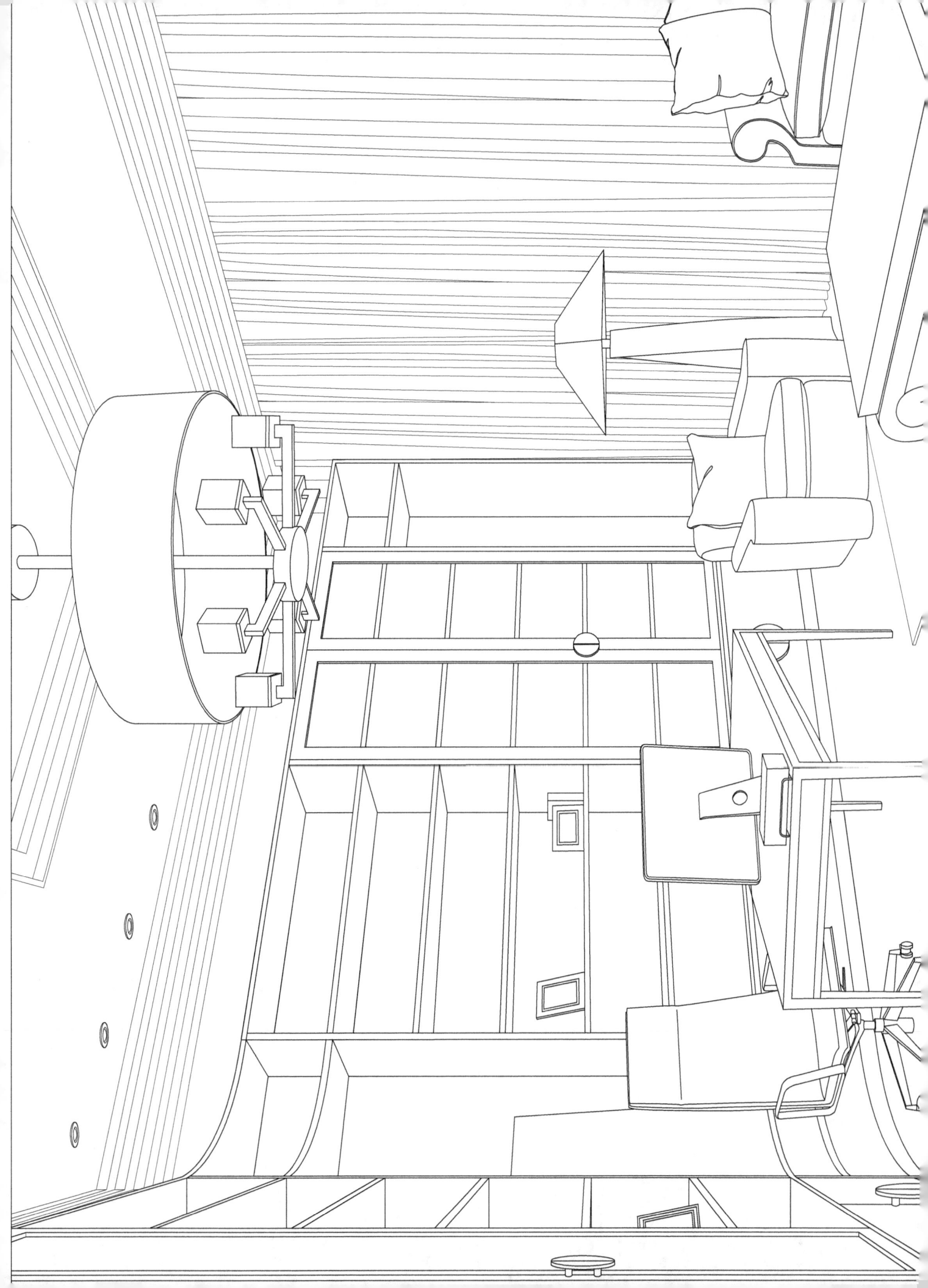

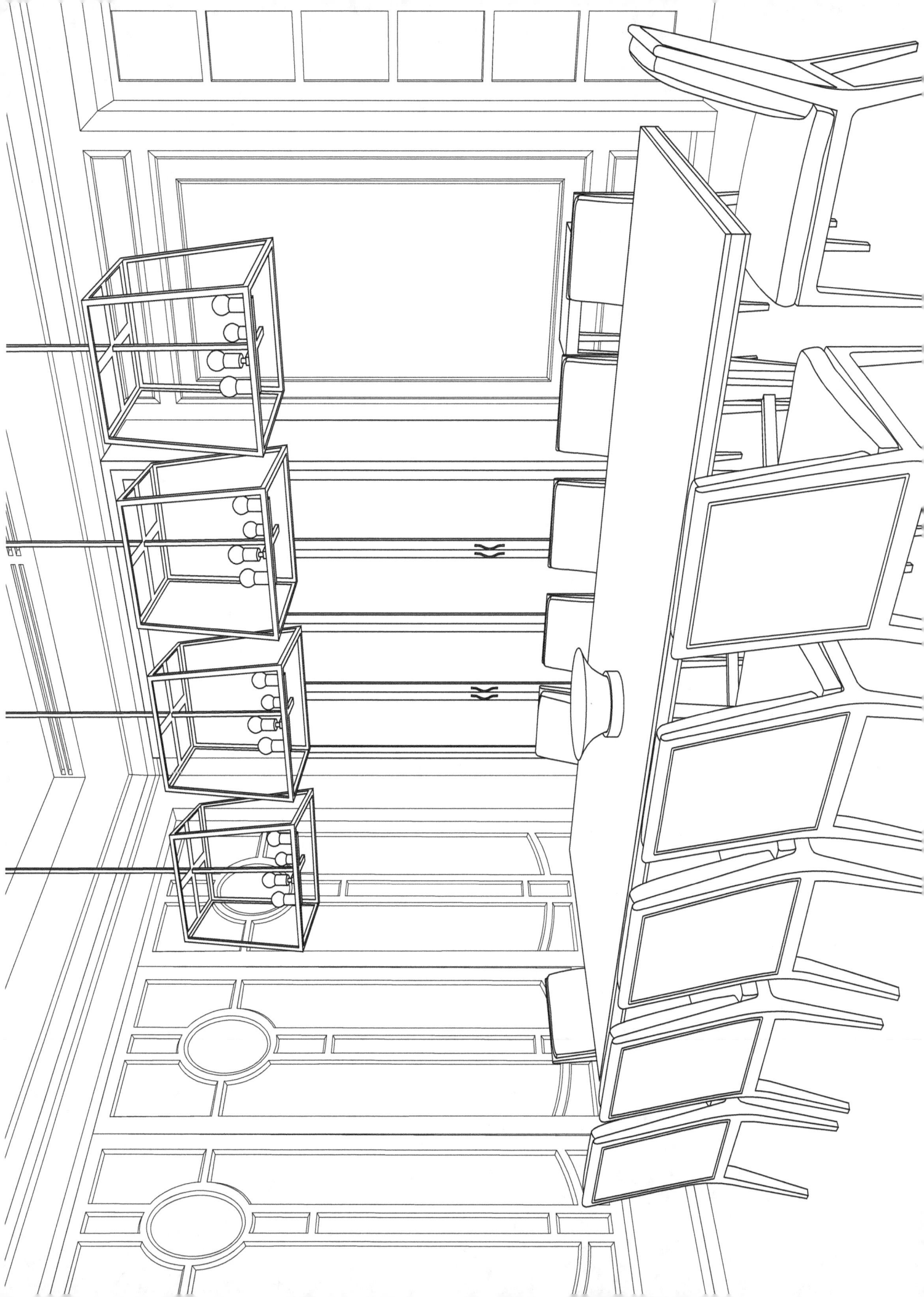

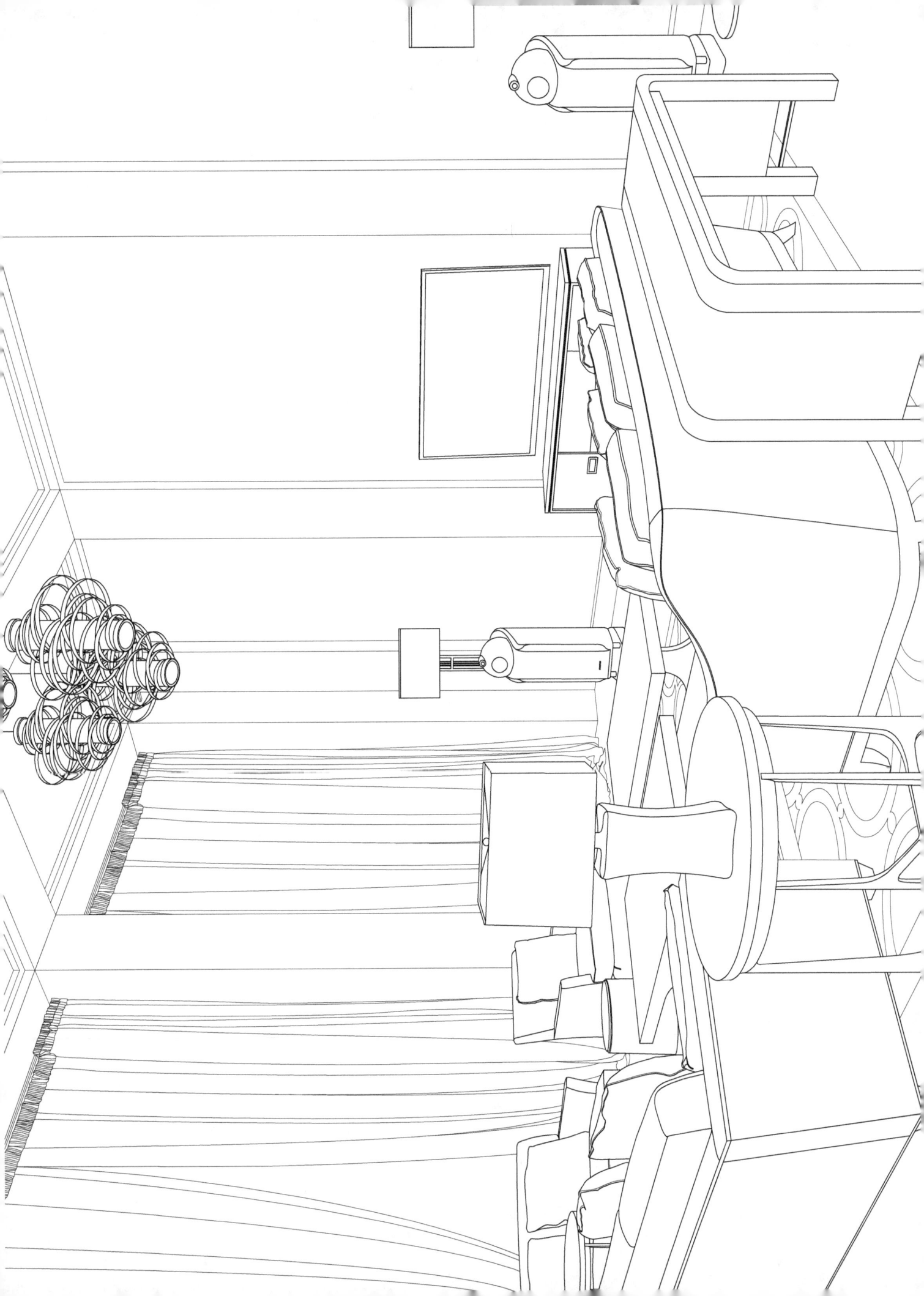

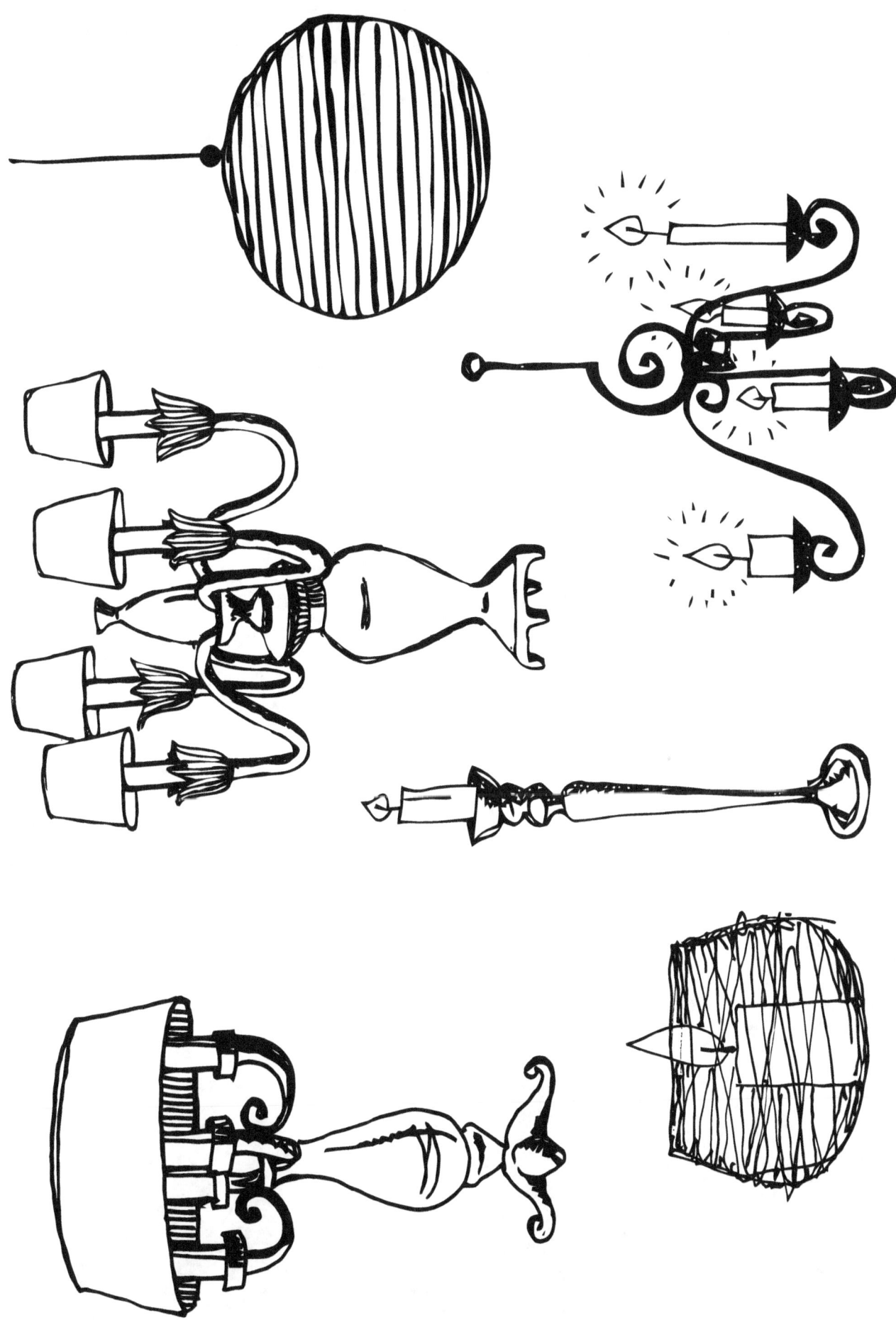

www.ingramcontent.com/pod-product-compliance
Lightning Source LLC
Chambersburg PA
CBHW081632220526
45468CB00009B/2406

* 9 7 8 1 9 0 8 7 0 7 5 1 2 *